Reflections of a **Horseman**

ART & TEXT BY JACK TERRY

Reflections of a Horseman

Text © 2001 by Jack Terry
Published by Blue Cottage Gifts™,
a divison of Multnomah Publishers, Inc.®
P.O. Box 1720, Sisters, Oregon 97759

ISBN 1-58860-026-2

Artwork © Arts Uniq'®, Inc.
Artwork designs by Jack Terry are reproduced under license from
Arts Uniq'®, Inc., Cookeville, TN, and may not be reproduced
without permission. For information regarding art prints featured
in this book, please contact:

    Arts Uniq'®, Inc.
    P.O. Box 3085
    Cookeville, TN 38502
    1-800-223-5020

Designed by Koechel Peterson and Associates, Minneapolis, Minnesota

Scripture quotations are taken from *The Ryrie Study Bible*, New American Standard
Translation © 1976, 1978 by The Moody Bible Institute; *The Holy Bible*, New International
Version (NIV) 1973, 1984 by International Bible Society, used by permission of Zondervan
Publishing House; *The Living Bible* (TLB) © 1971. Used by permission of Tyndale House
Publishers, Inc. All rights reserved.

Printed in China

01 02 03 04 05 06—10 9 8 7 6 5 4 3 2

www.bluecottagegifts.com

BLUE COTTAGE GIFTS™
OPEN THE DOOR TO JOY

DEDICATION

To my Grandparents, Bill and Maggie Mason,
who left such a precious heritage.

To Mom and Dad,
for preserving that great heritage.

And to my wife, Mary,
who is always right by my side.

TABLE
OF
CONTENTS

INTRODUCTION

"The horse is a creature who sacrifices his own being to exist through the will of another. He is the noble conquest of man."
BUFFON

The horse is one of the most valuable and endearing animals on earth. For thousands of years, horses have been a reliable source of transportation and companionship. They are highly intelligent, warm, and affectionate. They have performed heroic deeds, acted as beasts of burden, and remained loyally beside fallen soldiers in wartime. They have inspired artists and authors, raced in competitions, and stood silhouetted at the crests of buttes with strong, proud warriors astride. Their heritage is ancient.

For centuries, horses have pulled everything from chariots to covered wagons. They have plowed fields and led armies into battle. These noble beasts have carried explorers across our great continent and many a cowboy up a perilous trail.

A horseman, by definition, is either one who is skilled in riding a horse or one who owns, breeds, trains, or tends horses. However, regardless of whether you ride for pleasure or depend on horses for your livelihood, there are many life lessons to be learned from your equestrian companions. They are faithful to those who love them. They learn to trust those who are trustworthy. They are sensitive to the touch and the voice of their master. And for those of us who have spent a lifetime in their company, there is nothing like the relationship between a horseman and his steed.

If you own a horse, you understand the joy of walking into a barn and smelling the distinctive musky blend of horseflesh and leather...of laying your hand on a flank and feeling the ripple of a

muscle and the warmth of a body beneath your steed's glossy hide. You also realize that a horse is a great responsibility. And much like a child, it must be fed, washed, taught, and nurtured. You cannot stop the training at a halfway point and expect your horse to become intelligent, mature, and well behaved. He will not teach himself good habits, nor will he possess any great desire to please you unless he learns right from wrong. Although it takes a great deal of time, patience, and dedication, the rewards of an early morning ride on the back of an animal you know, love, and trust, make it worth every minute.

Because my Grandad was a cattleman, I became fascinated with horses at a young age. I don't claim to be a master horseman, but I have definitely learned many valuable lessons from working with horses. Like people, each one is different and has a distinct personality. Some are strong willed and stubborn. Others are compliant and willing. I've known a few to be accomplished Houdini's—managing to escape from stalls or corral gates on a regular basis. Each animal must be treated as a unique individual, with methods of training and handling him adjusted accordingly. The foundation for success is in building a relationship of trust. Just as we must learn to trust God and allow Him to guide our steps, the horse must likewise learn to trust his handler. The final objective is for the two to move together as one.

I invite you to ride along and enjoy a few tales of horsemanship in the poetry and prose of three generations of cowboys.

"A large and liquid eye...the swirl of dust around pounding hooves...these, then, are the images that move us."

ANONYMOUS

THE HORSEMAN'S LAST WISH

Being a Texan comes naturally to me since I am the fourth generation of Terry's to live in this great state. The love I have for the land and family was instilled in me in my formative years. The inspiration for much of what I paint today comes through the heart and remembrances of my Grandfather.

How well I remember the light in my Grandfather's eyes when he would settle in to spin a tale. If I watched and listened closely, he could transport me to a time many years past. We spent long hours together, he and I, with Granddad reminiscing and me glued to his stories. There were good guys and bad guys—but I had no doubt that my Granddad was always the hero. He was one of the last great cowboys…and how he loved to tell me about it…

Granddad was only three-years-old when he arrived in Texas. He rode in the back of a wagon with his brother and sister and his Grandma. His Daddy had searched long and hard for a spot to call home—a place where he could plow dirt, plant corn, and raise a family. Granddad told me he remembered hearing his Uncle Jim talking one time about this place called "Texas"—a place filled with wild mustangs running free, where land stretched for miles without a fence in sight!

My Great Grandfather fell in love with Texas as soon as he arrived there. Soon his family was settled into daily life. Granddad started school, and although he was about the smallest one in class, it didn't matter because he had already made up his mind about his

future. Granddad *knew* what *he'd* grow up to be! He had watched a friend's Daddy work on the Circle T—breaking broncs and chasing cattle—and he had it all planned! In a few years, he'd stop farming, quit school, and ride horses 'til their teeth rattled!

At the tender age of fifteen, Granddad moved away from home and got a job on a ranch. He mended fence, baled hay, and doctored cattle. It was there that he bunked in the barn and shared meals with his Mexican friend, Pedro. Before long, Granddad realized Pedro was likely the best horseman he would ever know. He had a way with horses that was almost magical. With a quiet voice and a gentle touch, he brought even the most ornery broncs under his gentle spell. Yes, Pedro was probably one of the first true "horse whisperers."

Granddad told me that, in the three years he lived on the ranch, he gained more knowledge than any college curriculum could have given him. He learned about living off the land, loving people, and treating animals with respect.

But Granddad still dreamed of life on the trail. God knew my Granddad's love for horses and understood the longing in his heart, so one day the Good Lord sent a friend out to the ranch to tell Granddad about a wrangling job on a cattle drive headed clear up to Missouri. Granddad knew it was his big chance, so he packed his gear, said his farewells, and rode off to follow his dreams.

For several years, Granddad learned firsthand about life on the trail. He rode trails that had earned reputations for turning boys into men—trails like the Chisholm, the Goodnight-Loving, and Western Trail. He spent long days and nights pushing horses and cattle through rain, dust, and snow, working his way to the railhead.

Then came the fierce winter of '87. It froze deep into cattle country, and many cows were lost. Cattle ranchers went broke, and Granddad's dream of the trail was over.

At first, Granddad leased a place and raised cattle and goats—with a sheep or two tossed in for good measure. He saved enough money to buy a sorrel stallion and a mare with a colt on the ground. He took a lot of pride in the quality of his horseflesh and soon gained a reputation for raising some of the finest horses in the Lone Star State.

Then one night my Granddad headed into town to go on a date with a girl named Maggie. It was love at first sight. He courted her all through the fall. Granddad told me she used to wait for him on her front porch and how he could see the gleam in her eye when he'd come calling.

He eventually bought a place of his own, and he and Grandma married when the house was finished that spring. They began to raise a family—four boys and two girls. One of those girls, Della, was my mother.

As time went by, my Grandparents' herd of horses grew, and so did their fine reputation. They needed more land. So Granddad bought the next ranch over, known as the "Little Lazy Seven." Granddad used to tell me, "How we loved that place! It was our own little piece of heaven."

One of the hardest times of my Granddad's life was during the 1930s when our country suffered the Great Depression. It hit folks hard in our part of the world. No one wanted to spend what little money they did have on horses. Granddad was forced to return to farming. By God's grace, he had learned how to farm early on, and he and his family were able to survive, and keep a few horses as well.

The family pulled together, and all four boys helped Granddad work the land. But times were changing, and ranching was becoming less profitable. Both of his girls grew up and went away to college. World War II called his three youngest sons away. But Bill, Granddad's oldest son, loved the ranch as much as he did, and stayed home to work the land side by side with his father.

Granddad said Bill was a natural with the land and a much better horseman than himself. As Bill's reputation grew, he was offered a good-paying job in Colorado with a cattle company and made the difficult decision to leave his family in pursuit of his dreams. His three brothers returned home from the war, and soon each married and began their own families. Granddad's ranch couldn't financially support the growing families and before long they all moved away, leaving Granddad and Grandma alone with their horses.

The Good Lord knew Granddad loved that ranch as much as life itself—and the heritage he'd built through drought and depression, as well as all the horses he'd trained and broken. But his heart wasn't strong, and the doctor said he couldn't run the place any more. So he and Grandma packed up their things and moved into town. At their new place Granddad had to have a barn so he could keep Old Dan, his bay gelding. It was a big red barn.

That's where I come into the story. It was in plain view of that barn that he and I spent long days together under the old mesquite tree, talking and watching the chickens scratch about in the yard. It was there that I heard tales about the Old West, tales about long-horns and trail drives, and bank robbers. Granddad saw the cowboy in me. He knew we were cut from the same cloth, he and I. It was he who bought me my first pony when I was five-years-old.

Granddad always told me that if he had just one wish, it would be to take me back to the ranch, and for us to run it together—just the two of us. And though we never actually got to do it, the joy and vision my Granddad gave me as we contemplated how it might be, were two gifts from him that have lasted me a lifetime.

STRAIGHT FROM THE HORSE'S MOUTH:

Proverbs 13:22 says, "A good man leaves an inheritance to his children's children." God wants us to preserve our heritage. He wants us to pass on our blessings from generation to generation. It is good to perpetuate the joy of loving one of His most faithful creatures—the horse. He also wants us to teach our children about the value of hard work and honesty. There are many legacies to hand down through the generations, but perhaps more valuable than money or land is the legacy of an example of a heart that is pleasing to God.

"...This most noble beast is the most beautiful, the swiftest, and of the highest courage of domesticated animals. His long mane and tail adorn and beautify him. He is of a fiery temperament, but good-tempered, obedient, docile, and well-mannered."

PEDRO GARCIA CONDE

A BOY'S CURIOSITY

"He doth nothing but talk of his horses."

WILLIAM SHAKESPEARE, THE MERCHANT OF VENICE

Grandad was a patient man. I tagged along behind most summer afternoons in West Texas, asking him all sorts of questions. We spent a lot of time around his old red barn. The dusty red sand blew tumbleweeds up against the barbed wire fence, where horn toads hunkered in the shade. His bay horse, Old Dan, stood in the corner, usually half asleep and resting one leg lazily off the parched ground. Chickens roamed the pasture and pens—clucking and scratching endlessly throughout the day.

A towering mesquite tree shaded the old barn. It forked at the base and was perfect for climbing. I often climbed out on its gnarled limbs and jumped onto the rusted tin roof of the barn while Grandad was doing his chores. I had to be very quiet, because he was always afraid I would fall off and break an arm or a leg. But as nature would have it, little boys can't be quiet for long. I found myself caught up in a make-believe gunfight with the bad guys, blurting out gunshot sounds until he finally summoned me down.

After chores were all finished, we would often sit and talk under the shade of that great tree. I enjoyed lying on my back, gazing up into the bright blue sky, and finding pictures of animals or faces in the clouds. One such afternoon I spotted a big puffy cloud shaped like a horse. I remember asking Grandad where we got our horses. As he glanced up into the sky at my horse cloud, he said, "God made them, son." That was not the response I was looking for, however. I had already learned about Noah's ark. I wanted to know how horses got to Texas. So Grandad began to

unfold to me the wonderful history of horses in our great state.

Grandad had been a cowboy all his life and had ridden on many cattle drives from South Texas to Kansas and Missouri. He loved the history behind the great King Ranch and their notoriously fine horses. He explained how the Spanish explorers came from Europe in their big ships and brought horses into Texas hundreds of years ago. He talked of how men like Mr. King and his family raised them and sold them to use on our ranches.

As his eyes gazed far out over the light powder blue mesas on the horizon, Grandad told how his father moved his family to Texas in a covered wagon pulled by four horses. He remembered when he and his dad plowed the cornfields with a horse, and on special occasions, often rode a buggy into town pulled by a big black horse they called "Pepper."

"But what about the cowboys, Grandad?" I exclaimed. About that time I heard the squeaky old screen door on the back porch open and Grandmother's call to get cleaned up for supper. When the aroma of her wonderful homemade bread, garden fresh vegetables, and juicy roast beef floated across the evening breeze, a fella didn't have to be told twice. I glanced back once

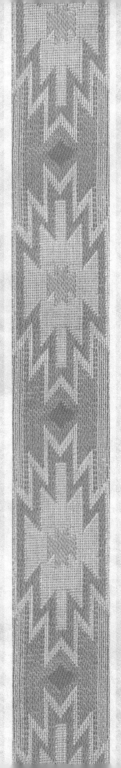

more at old Dan patiently standing in his stall...obviously awaiting his next bank robbery getaway. Oh well, the cowboys would just have to wait until another day.

STRAIGHT FROM THE HORSE'S MOUTH:

My Grandad was patient and attentive to my questions. I knew there would be another day when, once more, we would again sit under that old mesquite tree; when I would stare at old Dan and imagine myself riding on his back at a full gallop, or roping an errant steer on a cattle drive as Grandad continued the tales of his youth.

Children need to be heard and understood, but they can also learn a lot about patience and love from the elders in their lives if they are willing to listen. The lesson I learned from my Grandad on those long summer afternoons was the value of his endless interest and patience. He always made me feel so special and important, and that was an incredible legacy. I strive to have that gracious tolerance myself, and pray it will be something I, too, pass on to my own grandchildren.

King David said, "Listen, for I have worthy things to say" Proverbs 8:6.

Maybe we need to teach our children the value of the wisdom they can gain from the elder generation.

"Listen to your father, who gave you life, and do not despise your mother when she is old. Buy the truth and do not sell it; get wisdom, discipline, and understanding. The father of a righteous man has great joy; he who has a wise son delights in him. May your father and mother be glad; may she who gave you birth rejoice! My son, give me your heart and let your eyes keep to my ways."

PROVERBS 23:22-26

WHAT ABOUT THE COWBOYS?

"To make a perfect horseman, three things are requisite. First, to know how and when to help your horse. Secondly, how and when to correct him. And thirdly, how and when to praise him and to make much of him."

THOMAS BLUNDEVILLE

Little boys are a lot like horses. They have good memories. I wanted Grandad to tell me about cowboys, and I wouldn't stop pestering him until he did. He was very patient with me, enjoying a slower pace in his later years. That afternoon in the shade of the big mesquite, he shared a chapter out of his past.

By the age of fifteen, much to his father's chagrin, Grandad knew it was his calling to be a cowboy. His dad wanted him to stay and help him on the farm, but he didn't like planting corn. He longed to push cattle and break horses. So he left home and got his first job on a ranch in Central Texas. They had a lot of livestock and were also well known for their horses. The owner had three daughters and was getting up in years. He needed a strong back to help out. A Spanish family lived on the ranch, and Pedro helped break the horses. Grandad worked there a few years, living in a small room in the barn.

Pedro's kind family took him under their wing, feeding him most of his meals. He often bragged in later years of the wonderful beans and tortillas cooked each evening over an open fire. Pedro shared with him valuable training techniques perfected by his ancestors in Mexico. At that time, many horses were being broken using a rather harsh method that often broke the very spirit of the

horse in training. They would put a sack over his head, tie one of his hind legs up off the ground, and throw a saddle on. Then they would release the rope from the horse's leg and ride him until he could buck no more, due to complete exhaustion. This would generally break a horse to ride, alright, but he was broken in more ways than one, and it was virtually impossible to teach him beyond that point.

Pedro taught the horses to trust him and they became friends. Grandad was impressed by Pedro's gentle ways. He saw the difference those ways could make. Even as the horses submitted to Pedro's accomplished leadership, they were willing to do more for him. Willing to please. Willing to trust. Their intelligence was apparent. Grandad always loved a smart horse.

After about three years on that first job, a friend told him about a cattle drive that was leaving the King Ranch headed for the railhead in Abilene, Kansas. He felt that Pedro had turned him into a respectable horseman, and he was ready to pursue his dream of being a cowboy. He hired on and at the ripe old age of eighteen, he and his partner rode off to experience life on the open trail.

His talent with horses was soon recognized at the cow camp, and he was put in charge of the remuda of saddle horses for the drive. He made certain the horses were well fed and in good condition, and that each cowboy had a fresh mount for the new day.

Grandad rode up several long and dusty trails, including the Chisholm and Goodnight-Loving, until the severe winter of 1887 devastated the cattle in Texas—signaling the end of that great era in our history. The cowboys rode off in all directions. Some found jobs on ranches while others moved to the city. But horses ran deep in Grandad's veins. He would spend a lifetime scratching out a living off the dry West Texas land, much like the chickens that scratched endlessly around the barn now as he told me his stories.

I had enjoyed another lazy afternoon adventure with Grandad. But just as horses don't forget, I wasn't about to let go of the burning desire I held in my own heart....

"Grandad, I wanna be a cowboy just like you, but I don't even have a horse," I groaned.

"Hmmm," he replied softly, "We'll see what we can do about that." Just then the

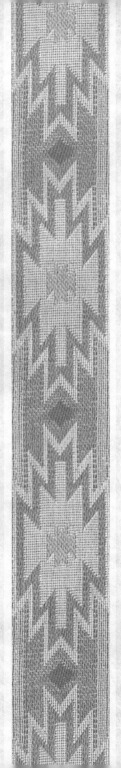

screen door opened. Supper was ready and—like clockwork—another afternoon in the shade of the mesquite tree was over.

STRAIGHT FROM THE HORSE'S MOUTH:

My Grandad was fortunate to realize his calling in life at a young age. He learned that gentle discipline is as healthy and necessary to the training of a good horse as it is to a good man.

He followed his heart, found favor with God, and had a good life. These words in Proverbs directed his steps:

> My son, never forget the things I've taught you. If you want a long and satisfying life, follow closely my instructions. Never forget to be truthful and kind. Hold these virtues tightly. Write them deep within your heart. If you want favor with both God and man, and a reputation for good judgment and common sense...don't ever trust yourself. In everything you do, put God first, and He will direct you and crown your efforts with success. Turn your back on evil. When you do that, then you will be given renewed health and vitality. (3:1–8, TLB)

These are words to hang your hat on.

"Do not be like the horse or the mule, which have no understanding, but must be controlled by bit and bridle or they will not come to you."

PSALM 32:9, NIV

MY FIRST HORSE

"How was a fellow supposed to be a cowboy when he didn't even have his own horse?" I pouted as I followed Grandad out to feed Old Dan. We had just returned from the Fourth of July parade downtown that hot summer afternoon, where I had ridden behind Grandad on the back of Old Dan, trailing along through the streets with the other horses and their riders. While I had a great time taking part in the parade, following along behind the floats and clowns, I found myself watching other young kids riding their horses alone. I guess I was a little jealous.

Still proudly wearing my new leather vest with silver conchos and matching chaps, new black boots with hand stitched red tops and jingling spurs, it was clear the only thing missing was a horse. I even had a shiny silver sheriff's badge pinned to my shirt and an official "Lone Ranger" imitation pearl-handled six-shooter strapped to my side. Yessir, there was only one thing I lacked.

Grandad went about his chores as I moped around kicking up dust with my new boots. I went outside and sat cross-legged on the ground under the big mesquite tree, resting my chin on my hands. A few minutes later, Grandad came out and sat down beside me. He said, "Son, you know a horse is a big responsibility. You have to give 'em food and water every day, and they have to be trained. Do you think you are big enough for that?"

"Sure am, Grandad," I replied. About that time we saw a truck coming up the long dirt road towing a horse trailer enveloped in a huge cloud of dust. We jumped up and went over to the house to see who it was.

While Grandad greeted the man at the pickup, I ran to the back of the trailer to see what Old Dan was whinnying about all the way from the barn. Tethered to the inside of the trailer was a beautiful gold Shetland pony with a long white tail and mane. There was a big red ribbon tied around her neck. I was so excited I couldn't speak a word. I just ran back up to the pickup jumping up and down trying to get Grandad's attention. He looked down and said, "Happy birthday, son."

The fact that it wasn't my birthday didn't even occur to me. I just remember yelling "Oh, boy!" and running to unload my new horse. When we got her to the barn, Grandad asked me what I was going to call her. I thought for a second and said, "Trigger. She looks just like Trigger." Roy Rogers and Trigger were my heroes, and I never missed their show on television. Finally, I was a cowboy with my very own horse.

That afternoon Grandad showed me how to put the halter on and tie her safely to the fence. We brushed her and combed her as she stood near Old Dan. They seemed to like each other, and I thought it was good that they were friends.

Grandad bought my mother a similar pony when she was a little girl. She used to

> "For a horse to trust you, you must trust the horse."
>
> ANONYMOUS

ride alongside Grandad and the other cowboys when they worked cattle in the pasture. Now it was my turn. I couldn't wait to ride out on Trigger. But Grandad said we had to wait for four weeks until I proved I could take care of her. He spent time every day teaching me many of the things he had learned so many years ago from Pedro. He taught me how to lead her, make her stop, back up, and stand still. We practiced saddling her with the same saddle my mother used on her horse, Patsy, many years before.

Four weeks seemed like an eternity, but finally it was time to saddle up and ride. Grandad stood by as I saddled Trigger. He helped tighten the cinch and make sure everything was properly fitted. My mother and grandmother stood proudly by as he gave me a leg up. Naturally, I was dressed in my full Roy Rogers attire—six-shooter and all! I proudly rode around the pen until everyone was thoroughly bored and Grandad finally had to pry me off of Trigger's back. It was almost time for supper, so the ladies went in the house while Grandad and I unsaddled and fed the horses. I begged to stay with Trigger awhile and promised to come in soon. Grandad conceded, but as soon as the screen door slammed, I became Roy Rodgers.

I slipped over and tied Trigger to the fence where she was eating, backed off about twenty paces, broke into a dead run, slapped my hands on her rump and tried to mount her bareback just like Roy did. I came up a little short and fell to the ground in a cloud of dust. Trigger turned around and looked at me like I had lost my mind, but went right on eating just the same. Undaunted by defeat, I got up, untied Trigger, and led her to the other side of the pen where I could get a longer run at her. I tied her to the fence, put her bit in, and draped the reins over her back for a quick getaway. I backed off about thirty paces this time, ran full speed, slapped her rump and jumped. Much to my surprise, I made it! I tapped her side, with my spurs to make our

first heroic run together, pulled my pearl-handled pistol from the holster, grabbed the reins, then realized I had not untied her lead rope from the fence.

About that time, Mother called from the back porch. It was getting dark and supper was waiting. The fun was over for today, but I had had my first glimpse of horsemanship. A bond of trust had already been established between Trigger and me in the few short weeks we had spent together. In all my craziness, she was never frightened. She knew we were friends. I think my Grandad knew a little something about the nature of horses—that it would be this way between us with a slow start.

STRAIGHT FROM THE HORSE'S MOUTH:

Children learn valuable lessons about the blessings that often come with additional responsibility. The gift I was given by my Grandad went far beyond the pony. It included firsthand understanding of the bonds of trust, and learning that trust is built by faith. It encompassed lessons in the joys of caring for a creature

you love. And it taught me a great deal about love and patience as Grandad worked alongside me day after day...and made me wait the longest four weeks of my life.

"No hour of life was lost spent in the saddle."

AUTHOR UNKNOWN

LIFE'S FIRST REAL TEST

"We have almost forgotten how strange a thing it is that so huge and powerful and intelligent an animal as a horse should allow another, and far more feeble, animal to ride upon its back."

PETER GRAY

For the next two summers, Grandad and I spent many an afternoon under the big mesquite tree by the barn. I was quite a horseman by now, and Trigger and I rode alongside Grandad and Old Dan for hours. We checked the windmills to make sure the stock had water, and rode the fence to see if any cows had broken a hole in the rusty old barbed wire. Sometimes we just stopped to look at the cows. Grandad got off of his horse, knelt down in the grass, pulled up a big long blade and just chewed on it for a while. I never really knew what he was thinking about because he never said a word. Not knowing what to do, I just did the same thing. We would sit there for hours. Then he would hop back in the saddle and off we'd go. I don't believe I ever saw him more contented. I too was content. I was finally living the life my young soul had always dreamed of.... I had my own horse, Trigger, and the next best thing to Roy Rogers to teach me about being a cowboy—my Grandad.

But one morning late that summer, just before school started, my mother told me we had to move away. Dad had a new job, and we had to go in a few days. "Don't worry," she said, "we'll come back and visit soon and you'll make lots of new friends."

I was old enough to see her choking back the tears and knew in my heart that I would not be back soon. "But what about Trigger?" I asked. "Can we take her with us?"

"Not right now, son. We don't have any place to keep her, and she will be better off here with Dan."

In a few days we were all loaded and driving off. I remember everyone hugging and trying hard to smile while holding back the tears. The last thing I remember seeing as we drove away was my Grandmother and Grandad standing in the dirt road almost obscured by the wake of dust from behind our car...waving good-bye. Behind them, in front of the old red barn I had come to love, Trigger stood alongside Old Dan. I felt like I had just lost my best friend. In just a few short weeks, I found out I had.

Grandad died suddenly of a heart attack that November, and Grandmother soon moved to a house in town. Everyone was so upset about everything that I kept my own worries to myself. But for weeks all I could think of was what might have happened to Dan and Trigger. Eventually I was assured they had a good home and a loving family to take care of them, but I was convinced my days as a cowboy were over. All I could do was dream.

And dream I did. Many were the nights I found myself at Grandad's side, listening anxiously for his next words about life on the trail. Together we swam mighty rivers

"He is pure air and fires and the dull elements of earth and water never appear in him, but only in patient stillness while his rider mounts him: he is indeed a horse..."

WILLIAM
SHAKESPEARE,
HENRY V

on our trusty steeds alongside a herd of longhorns that seemed to stretch all the way to Heaven. As hot branding irons were pulled from the fire, I smelled the stench of burning rawhide. I felt the chill of winter's first snow and the warmth of an orphan calf held close. Just before dawn, while sleeping near the campfire, I heard the faint cry of a coyote. When I awoke, the aroma of a grassy pasture filled my senses. It was then I knew what Grandad had been thinking about all those times he kneeled in the grass and gazed far past the light blue mesas on the horizon.

STRAIGHT FROM THE HORSE'S MOUTH:

Life is often a mystery to us. And the death of those we love always comes unbidden. Yet we each have a purpose. A destiny. Life is a gift from God, and we must make the most of it. My Grandad made the most of every day we had together. It was from him that I learned to treasure every moment of every hour. I learned it under the shade of the mesquite tree, always with Old Dan in clear view. It doesn't matter if we're young or old. Only by the revelation of a Holy God can we understand that our lives are gifts from Him, and that we must make the most of each waking moment.

King Solomon put it this way: "There is

an appointed time for everything. And there is a time for every event under heaven—A time to give birth, and a time to die" (Ecclesiastes 3:1-2.) The writer goes on to say, "I know that there is nothing better for them [man] than to rejoice and to do good in one's lifetime; moreover, that every man who eats and drinks sees good in all his labor—it is the gift of God" (v. 12-13).

Indeed, our lives are gifts. Let's make a difference.

"Here's to you, stocking and star and blaze.

You brought me all that the best could bring—

Health and mirth and the merriest days

In the open fields and the woodland ways—

And what can I do in return but sing

A song or two in your praise."

WILL OGILVIE

DREAMS OF A YOUNG HORSEMAN

"A horse already knows how to be a horse; the rider has to learn how to become a rider. A horse without a rider is still a horse; a rider without a horse is no longer a rider."

ANONYMOUS

I grew up without a horse of my own and so, as most little boys did, spent summers playing baseball and football in the vacant lot down the street with the other kids in the neighborhood. When we tired of sports, we retreated to my backyard, where we constructed a fort from old cardboard boxes and pretended to fight off the bad guys with our pistols—and a rifle we made from an old broom. But the greatest thrill of all was sneaking over the hill and through the deep weeds to where the rusty old railroad bridge towered above the creek on the edge of town. Perhaps it was so thrilling because our parents said it was too dangerous and forbade us to play there.

Every afternoon around four o' clock, we could hear the big train's whistle at the crossing about a mile before the bridge. We would just sit anxiously under the towering structure until someone would holler, "Look out, here she comes!" Then we'd all hold our ears as she screamed across the tracks high above us. The old bridge rattled so loudly I thought it was going to burst into a million rusty pieces and crush us all. As we got a little older, we grew braver and walked across the bridge to the other side, waiting until we heard the whistle. Then we ran as fast as horses from the gate to the other end and rolled down the hill, hiding in the deep, tall weeds...pretending to be robbers as we brandished our stick guns.

"To seek the wind's power, the rain's cleansing,
and the sun's radiant life, one need only look at the horse."

ANONYMOUS

One day I put a penny on the track to see what would happen when the big red and yellow locomotive ran over it. It flattened it into a piece of copper about the size of a quarter. I think that scared me a little, and I decided I didn't want to be flattened like my penny so I stopped waiting on the train. Instead, I went out in the morning, when I knew there was no train coming, grabbed a handful of rocks and sat in the middle of the bridge with my feet dangling off the side. As I pitched my rocks into the water I took pleasure in watching the horses graze in the pasture across the creek. I remember there was a big white one and a roan with a small colt beside her. My thoughts drifted back to Grandad's barn and all the wonderful afternoons we'd spent together talking about horses. I sat and daydreamed the mornings away, then dashed back home in time for lunch so my Mom wouldn't be too suspicious of where I'd been.

Very early on, I began to spend a great deal of time transforming my childhood memories and dreams into pictures. Everyone said I had a real talent for drawing, and it was a rewarding source of pleasure for me. I won first place in the county fair art show at the age of nine. The drawing was of Grandad's old cowboy boot, grouped with a cow skull and cactus. I discovered I could recreate my dreams and memories as an artist. The ranching heritage of my family was still very much alive somewhere deep within and itching to be captured on canvas.

Through my teen years, I pursued my art with great determination. I painted many scenes reflecting the tales I had heard at my Grandad's knee. Stories of the great cattle drives and campfires at the chuck wagon came to life with each new brush stroke. I rode horses as often as I could. My family spent many summers in Colorado visiting my aunt and uncle. My uncle was the manager of a feedlot that fed thousands of cattle daily. Our time together inspired many new paintings. I loved spending the

day with him on horseback— checking all
the cows and soaking up all the stories of
his life in the saddle.

At seventeen, I thought I knew about all
there was to know about horsemanship.
It seems young men about that age often
think more highly of themselves than
perhaps they should. I was never so
embarrassed as the day I was riding horses
with my girlfriend on her family's ranch.
No sooner had we ridden about a half mile
from the house when my horse decided it
would be much happier back at the barn,
reversed his path of travel, and bolted for
home at a dead run. As we ran beneath
towering oak trees, he was not deterred in
the slightest by my forceful pulls on the
reins. Since there was no stopping him, I
decided to save myself by lying forward
and plastering myself against his neck as
we raced under the thick, sturdy limbs of
the oak grove. As fate would have it, I
glanced up one limb too soon, and was
rewarded by a solid collision between an
unforgiving object and my forehead.

The next things I saw were brightly
colored stars floating randomly before my
eyes. I found myself prone in a field of yellow wildflowers and imagined I was dream-
ing when I heard the dainty little words, "I
thought you knew how to ride." My ego
was crushed. It was all too obvious to

"No one can teach
riding better
than a horse."

ANONYMOUS

everyone that I was less than the horseman of my dreams. The massive scrape across my forehead reminded me of that horrific fact each time I looked in the mirror for the next several weeks. The experience, however, was a valuable one. I learned that sometimes there is a vast difference between our dreams and reality. While I had dreamed for many years of being a great horseman, I lacked the experience to make it a reality. I also dreamed of being a serious artist, but soon discovered I had a lot to learn about the reality of the professional world. I wasn't certain what the future held in store, but I knew deep down inside that I was destined to pursue both dreams with all my heart.

> "A man on a horse is spiritually, as well as physically, bigger than a man on foot."
>
> JOHN STEINBECK

STRAIGHT FROM THE HORSE'S MOUTH:

We can either view life as horses at the starting gate or like a flattened penny on the railroad track. God wants us to experience victory. He wants us to be excited when the gate opens and we hear the starting gun. When we get thrown off our horse in the race of life, God wants us to view those times as learning experiences that will make us stronger, rather than as giant trains that crush us in defeat like pennies on the track. "Consider it all joy, my brethren, when you encounter various trials, knowing that the testing of your faith produces endurance. And let endurance have its perfect result, that you may be perfect and complete, lacking in nothing" James 1:2-4.

So, what are you waiting for? Get up, dust yourself off, and head for the starting gate. Try again.

"His neck is high and erect, his head replete with intelligence, his belly short, his back full, and his proud chest swells with hard muscle...It is a most absolute and excellent horse."

POLYDORE VERGIL

LIFE IN THE REAL WORLD

"When I bestride him, I soar. I am a hawk. He trots the air; the earth sings when he touches it. The basest horn of his hoof is more musical than the pipe of Hermes."

WILLIAM SHAKESPEARE, HENRY V

Between high school graduation and the beginning of college, I spent three excruciatingly long months working in the Texas oil fields. My Dad thought it would be good for me to experience life as he had known it for twenty-five years. It was the longest, hardest, hottest, and dirtiest three months of my life—and I swore I would go to school year-round to avoid that again. And that's exactly what I did. I finished college in three years, attending both summer sessions between semesters.

I was determined to pick myself up out of the pasture where that horse had gotten the better of me at seventeen and exchange my adolescent dreams for reality. Soon after graduation, I moved to a ranch in West Texas, where I lived and worked for ten dollars a day, with room and board provided. It was a wonderful experience, and the ten dollars came in handy to a starving artist. I worked with horses almost every day for four years—while painting and showing my work in art galleries throughout the state. Those years instilled in me a love for the land and an admiration for people who worked with honesty and integrity for entire lifetimes, receiving little more than peace and contentment as their reward. I have come to understand that those qualities are the most valuable possessions we can have.

One of my memorable lessons in horsemanship came at the

"Where would we be without the horse?" It is kind of like asking, "What would seeds do without the wind?"

ANONYMOUS

hands of a Native American friend from a neighboring ranch. His peaceful way with horses reminded me of my Grandad's. We spent many uncounted evenings huddled around a campfire, strumming old cowboy ballads on our guitars, talking about horses and life on the open range. There was an ancient Indian burial ground just over the hill on a cliff overlooking the river. As he shared the history and traditions of his ancestors, a breeze screeched eerily through the giant pecan trees, adding a greater dimension to the stories he shared.

Early Native Americans, he explained, believed that a special relationship existed between man and animals—and that the two frequently communicate. Horses, in particular, were often man's companions, best friends, and teachers. Through that relationship of trust, the two rode as one. Horses ran in large, wild herds across our continent for hundreds of years and, by nature, that "herd mentality" remains fixed in them. My friend explained how herd animals learn to respect the dominant leader and said that, when working with a horse, I should imagine us as a "herd of two" in which I should always assume the dominant leadership role...speaking very softly, very quietly.

My friend said horses have feelings and are certainly able to think and respond to what they are being taught. They also have great memories, and it is much easier to train a horse properly from the beginning than to get your horse to unlearn bad habits later. "Always remember a horse would rather run than fight, so speak softly, build trust, and you will have a friend for life," he said. Much of my Indian friend's wisdom is echoed by other true "horse whisperers" today.

Everything we teach our horses can be applied to our own lives. Building friendships with people requires the application of about the same principles as horse training. Like horses, people need to hear a gentle voice in the noise of today's world. We need to devote our time and energies to those we care about. It is important to be patient and understanding. And when we develop relationships built on trust, we make friendships that last a lifetime.

STRAIGHT FROM THE HORSE'S MOUTH:

I want to close with a brief excerpt from a letter I received from my friend, Shay Cowden. She is a special woman, who has devoted much of her life to loving and caring for her horses. Anyone who has lost a horse or a special pet will relate to her story...

"I rocked her, and thanked God for sharing her splendor with us...and prayed for Him to take her home. I hate illness and seeing death, but I could not leave this special angel. I felt I was given a gift to be able to touch one of God's babies for a few hours and feel closer to Him. We are all so rushed in our lives. No extra minutes. But, what if we all took just a few minutes every day to try and find a way to love one of God's children? What could that mean to an angry child in their future? I am learning the meaning of the words patience, consistency, and frustration. I am overcoming fears and growing stronger. I see God's love in His creations, feel peace when I pet His animals, and my heart soars

"His is a power enhanced by pride, a courage heightened by challenge. His is a swiftness intensified by strength, a majesty magnified by grace. His is a timeless beauty touched with gentleness, a spirit that calls our hearts to dream."

ANONYMOUS

when I watch my horses run just for the joy of it. We are all the same. The beauty of His love is in all of us. Horses are blessed by His love, and are so beautiful when they run with such freedom."

My friend is right. Our lives in the real world are begging us to remember, "The beauty of His love is in all of us." It is a truth we often do not see or, in our "humanness," that we often misunderstand.

"If you ride a horse, sit close and tight,
if you ride a man, sit easy and light."

BENJAMIN FRANKLIN

FRIENDSHIP

As I sit in the shade of a towering mesquite,
Alone in the breeze, finding rest from the heat,
I gaze at the clouds in the blue sky above.
My mind floats away to the days I loved...

Gettin' older now, but I have a good life.
I cowboy, break horses, paint pictures...have a wonderful wife.
We raised two daughters on this ranch we call home,
Have four grandkids and two more sons I now call my own.

I was still wet behind the ears when I learned to break horses—
never liked to treat 'em rough, gave 'em lots of choices.
Just like people, horses—they're all different you see.
What works for you may not work for me.

We first work on trust a few minutes each day,
I lead 'em and work 'em...then give 'em some hay.
We soon become friends, my ponies and me—
A strong bond of trust, you see—that's the key.

I teach 'em patience and the feel of the bit;
to have a soft mouth, it must be a perfect fit.
Then comes the blanket and saddle on their back,
I tighten the cinch, hear the creak of the tack.

The first ride is fun 'cause some horses will buck...
Most will just sit there; never think it's just luck.
We ride every day 'til the lessons are done.
In just a few weeks then, the two ride as one.

I've befriended many horses folks said could never be broke.
Guess it's a gift the Lord gave to this old cowpoke.
I think the world still has a lot it hasn't learned...
You see trust can't be bought; it has to be earned.

So I'll teach my grandkids, like Grandad taught me.
A horse can be the best friend that you'll ever see.
Just be gentle and kind and full of respect,
'Cause friendships can be lost sometimes due to neglect.

STRAIGHT FROM THE HORSE'S MOUTH:

As we watch a horse running with full abandon, in total freedom,
through a field of flowers, we may see with our eyes but not really
understand why we feel such envy. Jesus said in John 8:32, "and
you shall know the truth and the truth shall make you free."

God, in His infinite love, has given each of us the choice to be free. Free from sorrow and pain. Free from anger and hatred. Free to choose to seek His love. Free to love one another. We are reminded of this incredible love by the endless detail we see in His animal kingdom—intricate patterns covering the pinions of His glorious birds...skins and scales that camouflage and protect other creatures from predators. Yes, there is marvelous color and hue throughout His prized domain. But He seems to have given special attention to the magnificence of the horse. Rippling muscles under slick leather hide, mane and tail unfurled, running with the wind—free to be who God created him to be.

We, too, can be free to be who God meant us to be. And this is a freedom like no other....

Look back at our struggle for freedom,

Trace our present day's strength to its source,

And you'll find that man's pathway to glory

is strewn with the bones of the horse.

ANONYMOUS